HOW SETUP YOUR KINDLE FIRE HD

A Complete Beginner to Pro Guide on
How To Set Up Your Kindle Fire HD into
Kindle Devices in less than 5 minutes

BY

WILLIAM MARK
Copyright©2017

COPYRIGHT

TABLE OF CONTENT

CHAPTER 1

INTRODUCTION

Kindle fire HD is one of the most popular device with lots of exciting features, the kindle fire is one of the latest addition to Amazon.com kindle family of devices, kindle fire is the first device from Amazon to move beyond eBook reading also provide a full tablet experience with a multitouch display screen with the ability to watch movies, read books, and play music also install applications from Amazon app store.

If you bought your Kindle fire and you are really in need of a guide to teach you how to setup some setting, there is no need to worry. This guide will educate you on how to set up your kindle fire get started.

we'll walk you through by setting up the reading, gaming, video and some apps on your tablet you got by turning on security and guidelines on how to use your fire HD and set it up with 5 minutes.

It is necessary to provide a great Kindle Fire HD case to protect your new device.

CHAPTER 2

KINDLE FIRE HD SETUP

Kindle Fire HD guides users on steps to take on the setup, be prepaid to take the instructions.

Choose your language, you can change your language when you choose to do so but is advisable to choose one language to avoid confusion. Turn on your WIFI and connect to a home network enter the password if necessary.

Now login to your Amazon account, if you bought the Kindle Fire HD from another account you wish to use it will set up. If you received it as a gift, you will definitely need to change it to your own account. It keeps your data and purchases in sync. Chose your time zone and confirm your Amazon account. The Kindle Fire HD then prompt you to set up facebook and twitter accounts. It makes is easy to share updates on social media. To see updates on facebook and twitter users you need to download the apps and enter your username and password.

CHAPTER 3

KINDLE FIRE HD SECURITY

To protect your Kindle Fire HD from others not accessing your Amazons purchases, read your email and access your apps it's best to set a password on your kindle fire HD.
 To set password follow this steps.
1. Click on settings
2. Click on security
3. Lock screen password on.
 Type pin or password of your chose
Parental Controls
It's a good idea to set up parental controls on the kindle fire if you'll be sharing with a kid.

1. Pull down from the top of the screen and click more on the right.

2. Click parental controls and click on

3. Choose a password, that is quite different from the device password.

Parents can control app purchases video playback, web browsing and email and more with the use of toggles like these below.

The kindle Fire HD accepts free Time, a way of allowing kids to use some apps and perform select activities for a limited amount of time.

Click and open the Apps for the kindle free time.
Click and open the app and create a password.

Add a profile. Choose a name and photo for the account. Kindle Fire HD supports up to 6 profiles.

Parents can manage and control the content, apps, books, and movies to a child's account.

Screen time limits can be monitored by opening the Kindle Free time app by moving down from the free time app and clicking on more. Input the free time password now tap on set daily time limits. Parents can equally set the screen time for a profile and a particular content activity times to permit for unlimited reading, but only per hour of apps as one example.

CHAPTER 4

USING THE KINDLE FIRE HD

Visit Amazon app store to install apps. The kindle Fire permits users to swipe through apps, books and videos on the home screen.

Setting up Email

1. To use email on the Kindle Fire HD, pull down from the screen,then click on more.
2. Click on application
3. Click on email, contact, calendars
4. Add an Account.
5. Enter username and password for popular accounts or fill in details for the other accounts.

The Kindle Fire HD will be set up for email, contacts and calendar events.

CHAPTER 5

OTHER TIPS AND TRICKS TO KNOW

Now you'll be guided through some hints to get started   with your kindle fire HD, content linked to your device, or apps from the Amazon app store they downloaded the off.

Your kindle books will show in the carousel automatically, along with the latest apps and any other downloaded content.

To delete items from the carousel, click and hold to book cover and delete from carousel.

If you wish to add books to favorite, click and hold, then click add to favorite. You can view your favorite by clicking the star icon at the bottom right of the screen.

Install apps that are saved, click on the cloud tab, click on any icon to start the app downloading into your device.

To import music collection, you'll have to
set up Amazon cloud player on your tablet
visit this site
http://www.amazon.com/gp/dmusic
/marketing/CloudPlayerLaunchPag
e at your device to start importing the
music from your computer cloud player,
you can now be able to streamed or
downloaded into your Kindle Fire HD.

THE END

William Mark

William Mark

William Mark

William Mark